FunTime® Piano

Classics

REVISED EDITION

Level 3A – 3B

Easy Piano

This book belongs to: _____

Arranged by

Nancy and Randall Faber

Production Coordinator: Jon Ophoff
Design and Illustration: Terpstra Design, San Francisco
Engraving: Dovetree Productions, Inc.

FABER
PIANO ADVENTURES®
3042 Creek Drive
Ann Arbor, Michigan 48108

A NOTE TO TEACHERS

FunTime® Piano Classics offers the elementary pianist arrangements of some of the great masterworks of Western music. The pieces, drawn primarily from symphonic and operatic literature, were carefully selected for their special appeal to students.

The *Classics* books are available in all levels of the *PreTime® to BigTime® Piano Supplementary Library,* and offer the piano student a wonderful opportunity to become familiar with these famous works.

FunTime® Piano Classics is part of the *FunTime® Piano* series. "FunTime" designates Level 3 of the *PreTime® to BigTime® Piano Supplementary Library* arranged by Faber and Faber.

Following are the levels of the supplementary library, which lead from *PreTime®* to *BigTime®*.

PreTime® Piano	(Primer Level)
PlayTime® Piano	(Level 1)
ShowTime® Piano	(Level 2A)
ChordTime® Piano	(Level 2B)
FunTime® Piano	(Level 3A-3B)
BigTime® Piano	(Level 4-above)

Each level offers books in a variety of styles, making it possible for the teacher to offer stimulating material for every student. For a complimentary detailed listing, e-mail faber@pianoadventures.com or write us at the mailing address bellow.

Visit **www.PianoAdventures.com**.

Helpful Hints:

1. Hands-alone practice is often helpful when learning a piece.

2. The songs can be assigned in any order, although the last two pieces in the book are somewhat more challenging.

3. Students should be encouraged to listen to recordings of the selections. This will enhance their conception and performance of the pieces while preparing them to be appreciative concertgoers.

About the Classics

A "classic" is a work of art or literature that is generally recognized to be of the highest quality. Many works of art were popular in their day, but later forgotten. A classic, however, withstands the test of time—it endures to be appreciated and enjoyed by later generations.

ISBN 978-1-61677-022-8

Copyright © 1990, 2010 by Dovetree Productions, Inc.
c/o FABER PIANO ADVENTURES, 3042 Creek Dr., Ann Arbor, MI 48108
International Copyright Secured.   All Rights Reserved.   Printed in U.S.A.

TABLE OF CONTENTS

Pomp and Circumstance

Sir Edward Elgar
(1857-1934)

Broadly

Eine Kleine Nachtmusik

Wolfgang Amadeus Mozart
(1756-1791)

Blue Danube Waltz

Johann Strauss, Jr.
(1825-1899)

Moderate waltz tempo

In the Hall of the Mountain King
(from *Peer Gynt Suite*)

Edvard Grieg
(1843-1907)

Crisp march tempo

Theme from The "Unfinished" Symphony

Franz Schubert
(1797-1828)

Allegro moderato

Toreador's Song
(from the opera, *Carmen*)

Georges Bizet
(1838-1875)

Waltz

Johannes Brahms
(1833-1897)

18

Theme from Peter and the Wolf

Sergei Prokofiev
(1891-1953)

Musetta's Song
(from the opera, *La Bohème*)

Giacomo Puccini
(1858-1924)

Light Cavalry Overture

Franz von Suppé
(1819-1895)

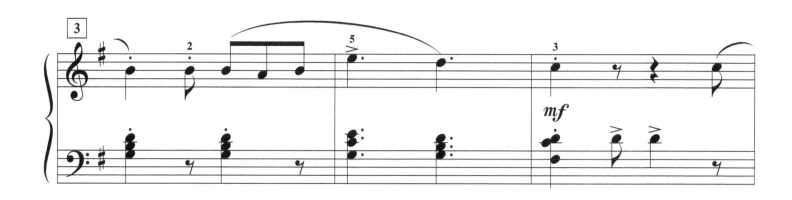

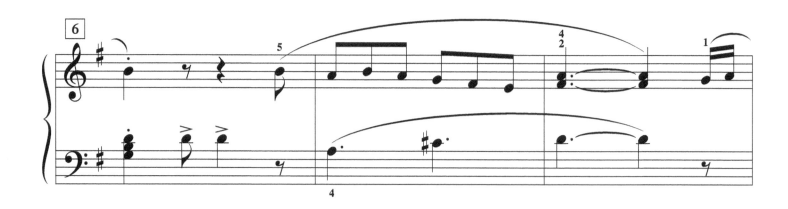

Theme from Scheherazade

Nicolai Rimsky-Korsakov
(1844-1908)

26

Dance of the Sugar Plum Fairy
(from the ballet, The Nutcracker)

Peter Ilyich Tchaikovsky
(1840-1893)

*Pedal optional

Overture to The Barber of Seville

Gioacchino Rossini
(1792-1868)

sempre staccato

DICTIONARY OF CLASSICAL TERMS

Ballet   Musical theater which uses dance to tell a story. Besides dance, ballet uses music, scenery and costumes (but no singing).

Opera   A drama set to music, with singing, acting and, sometimes, dancing. In an opera, the characters express themselves by singing instead of speaking.

Overture   An orchestral piece which begins an opera. The overture usually contains themes heard later in the opera.

Suite   A set of short pieces, often written in dance forms.

Symphony   A major composition for orchestra. A symphony has several sections called *movements* (usually four).

Theme   The main melody of a composition. (Many works have more than one theme.)

Waltz   A dance in 3/4 time. Waltzes have continued to be popular from the 1800's to today.